My Five Super Senses
I SEE IT!

Theresa Emminizer

PowerKiDS press

I use my eyes to see things!

I see bright colors!

I see different shapes.

I see myself!

I look happy.

9

I see my friends' faces.
They are beautiful!

I see the stars.
They shine!

I see clouds in the sky.

I see the snow
falling down.

I see my bunny.

She sees me too!

19

I see my food.
It looks good!

21

I see the sun
going down.

Published in 2024 by The Rosen Publishing Group, Inc.
2544 Clinton Street, Buffalo, NY 14224

First Edition

Editor: Theresa Emminizer
Book Design: Rachel Rising

Photo Credits: Cover, p. 1 TinnaPong/Shutterstock.com; p. 3 JGA/Shutterstock.com; p. 5 Dmytro Zinkevych/Shutterstock.com; p. 7 Alena Zolot/Shutterstock.com; p. 9 Pixel-Shot/Shutterstock.com; p. 11 wavebreakmedia/Shutterstock.com; p. 13 KIDSADA PHOTO/Shutterstock.com; p. 15 Pete Pahham/Shutterstock.com; p. 17 Irina Wilhauk/Shutterstock.com; p. 19 narikan/Shutterstock.com; p. 21 chingyunsong/Shutterstock.com; p. 23 Alex_Maryna/Shutterstock.com.

Library of Congress Cataloging-in-Publication Data

Names: Emminizer, Theresa, author.
Title: I see it! / Theresa Emminizer.
Description: New York : PowerKids Press, [2023] | Series: My five super
    senses | Audience: Grades K-1
Identifiers: LCCN 2023032677 (print) | LCCN 2023032678 (ebook) | ISBN
    9781499443356 (library binding) | ISBN 9781499443349 (paperback) | ISBN
    9781499443363 (ebook)
Subjects: LCSH: Vision--Juvenile literature. | Eye--Juvenile literature. |
    Senses and sensation--Juvenile literature.
Classification: LCC QP475.7 .E46 2023 (print) | LCC QP475.7 (ebook) | DDC
    612.8/4--dc23/eng/20230726
LC record available at https://lccn.loc.gov/2023032677
LC ebook record available at https://lccn.loc.gov/2023032678

Manufactured in the United States of America

Some of the images in this book illustrate individuals who are models. The depictions do not imply actual situations or events.

CPSIA Compliance Information: Batch #CWPK24. For further information contact Rosen Publishing at 1-800-237-9932.

Find us on